Life's Greatest Values

Life's Greatest Values
Persons in Relationship

By Paul C. Heubach

Southern Publishing Association, Nashville, Tennessee

In addition to the King James Version of the Bible, the following versions have been quoted:

The Bible: A New Translation, by James Moffatt. Copyright, 1954. Reprinted by permission of Harper & Row, Publishers, Inc.

The New Testament in Modern English. Copyright, J. B. Phillips, 1958. Used by permission of The Macmillan Company.

Copyright © 1976 by Southern Publishing Association. SBN 8127-0121-6. This book was edited by Richard Coffen and designed by Dean Tucker. Cover illustration is by Michael Sloan. Printed in U.S.A.

Contents

Life's Greatest Values 7

Understanding Ourselves 13

Selfishness Versus True Self-fulfillment 19

Relationships Begin in the Home 26

What Is Love? 30

No Love Without Communication 47

Life's Blessings Are Mediated
   in the Context of Fellowship 53

The Heart of Christianity 61

Life's Greatest Values

On a hillside somewhere in old Saxony is a cave filled with treasures, according to an old legend. The door to the cave is locked, and the key lies buried in the ground nearby. Occasionally a rare little flower grows over the key, and anyone recognizing the flower could dig around and find the key. Should he then discover the cave, he might enter and claim all the treasures he could carry home.

A little boy herding his father's sheep on the hills and in the valleys nearby found the flower one day. Remembering the legend, he dug around, found the key, then searched for the cave. Upon discovering it, the boy found that the key fit the lock. He opened the door, and as soon as his eyes became accustomed to the darkness, lo and behold, there they were—treasures abundant. The tables overflowed with them. They hung on the walls, and some even dangled from the ceiling. Realizing that all he could carry out would be his, he filled his pockets and his shirt and his cap and his arms with what he considered to be the most valuable items.

As he turned for the door, a voice startled him. "Take what you like, Son," said the voice, "but don't forget the best." Thinking that perhaps he had missed something worthwhile, he put the treasures back and for the second time filled his pockets, his shirt, his cap, and his arms with what he thought might be of even more value. As he made for the door, again the voice spoke. This time it sounded more insistent. "Take what you like, Son, but don't forget the best." He looked to the rear of the cave, and there he saw a little old man seated on a stool. Reassured by the old man's kindly face, the shepherd boy decided to try once more. For the third time he selected very carefully what he thought was of most value. As he staggered, heavily laden, toward the door, sure enough, for the third time—this time most insistently—the little old man urged, "You may take what you like, Son, but why don't you take the best?" What should he do? He had selected as wisely as he knew. He didn't know what would be of greater value. So he decided to be satisfied with what he had, and he went out.

By this time the sun had set, and it was beginning to get dark. The boy hadn't gone far when suddenly his heavy treasures became as light as a feather. As he examined them in the

Life's Greatest Values

twilight, he found they were nothing but dry, worthless leaves.

For a long time I didn't like that story. If what seems valuable turns out not to be, what can one do? The boy tried to choose the best. If in the sunset of life and after three careful attempts what one sincerely thinks is of real value turns out to be nothing but dry, worthless leaves, how can one be sure of anything? What is worthwhile in life? What are life's greatest values?

Actually, nothing has value except in relationship.

Consider, for example, a living cell. A single, living cell is a marvelous little piece of machinery. In grade school we learned that a cell consists of three parts: a membrane, a blob of protoplasm, and a nucleus. Now, of course, we realize there is far more to a cell than that. The membrane itself contains little pumps, or cytes, which force in and out certain chemicals. In fact, that membrane itself is an outstanding little computer. The blob of protoplasm is also complicated. The protein molecule in it is ponderous, and the chromosomes and genes also have many parts. All the parts of the cell in relationship form a very valuable little bit of life—more valuable than any of the parts alone.

But even a tiny cell alone has little value

unless it is associated with other cells to form a tissue. Tissue is of more value when associated with other tissues in an organ. And in turn, the organ itself would be of no value unless associated with other organs to make up a system. Finally, one system in relationship to other systems makes up the marvelous body.

Persons in Relationship

Even persons were not made to be alone. We were made to enjoy fellowship with one another and with our Creator-God. Therefore, I would like to submit as a basic theme for this little booklet that life's greatest values are persons in relationship.

When it comes to persons in relationship, attitudes and motives are most important. Words and actions are perhaps next. Have you noticed that some people can say certain things to you, and it somehow almost makes your blood boil, whereas others may say the same words, and you like it? Why? What makes the difference? The attitudes and motives involved. Therefore attitudes and motives are even more important than words or actions.

As important as we think they are, *things* are really least important when it comes to relationships. Yet how often *things* loom largest on our horizon. Things were made for persons, not persons for things. Too many of us love things and use persons, when it ought to be the other way around. We should love persons and use things. What if you had all your lover's gifts of things, but someone else had your lover?

In fact, things have spoiled many human relationships. Perhaps you've seen brothers become lifelong enemies over the settlement of an estate. It seems that we take a long time to discover that "a man's life consisteth not in the abundance of the things which he possesseth" (Luke 12:15).

Coming back, then, to the little shepherd boy in the legend, what was wrong with his choices? What should he have done differently? It seems to me that his whole sense of values revolved around *things*. How much better if he had talked to the little man on the stool. First, he could have asked, "What do you mean by 'the best'?" He could have invited the little old man home for dinner. He might then have had access to all the treasures in the cave. Obviously it is only a legend, but the originator of the story wanted to tell us that life's greatest values are not things but persons. And I would add the words *in relationship*.

Jesus taught that persons are more important than anything else in all the world. "What shall a man give in exchange for his soul?" He asked in Mark 8:37. "What shall it profit a man, if he shall gain the whole world, and lose his own soul?" (verse 36). To lose your soul is to lose yourself, and you are of inestimable value.

Persons are even more important than doctrine. Remember Jesus declared, "The sabbath was made for man, and not man for the sabbath" (Mark 2:27). The apostle Paul wrote that faith, hope, and love are the three most abiding realities in life, and that the greatest of these is love (1 Corinthians 13:13). These three virtues have no real significance apart from persons. *Persons* believe, *persons* hope, and *persons* love. And they have faith in, hope for, and love of other people.

That which brings us the greatest happiness also can bring us the greatest sorrow. Indeed our capacity for happiness and our capacity for sorrow are identical. Yet again most experiences in life that bring us the greatest happiness as well as those that bring us the greatest sorrow have to do with human relationships. Because this is true, it is important to learn how to establish the right love relationship with persons.

Understanding Ourselves

When it comes to personal human relationships, it is important that we understand ourselves. The difficulty we have in relating to people lies largely within ourselves, for what we think of ourselves has a great deal to do with what we think of others. When self-respect wanes, respect for others lessens too. We tend to think that others are as bad as we are.

To improve our interpersonal relationships then, we should begin with ourselves and seek to understand why we do what we do and why we react as we do to others. Why is it that some people appeal to us and others repel us? Which is the greater motivation, knowledge or emotions? Why is it we do some things we know we shouldn't and don't do some things we know we should? I think we all recognize that our likes and dislikes have a great deal to do with how we behave.

All our desires have their roots in God-given basic needs. For example, why do we crave a cool refreshing drink on a hot day?

Obviously it is because we need it in our system. God made us that way. Why do we get hungry at certain times? The desire for food is rooted in the basic need for nourishment. Again, God made us that way.

At the risk of oversimplification, let us list six basic human needs in which all our desires are rooted: spiritual, aesthetic, meaning, acceptance, self-realization, and physical.

Beginning with the bottom of the list, we have physical needs. Besides the need for food and water, mentioned previously, we also need fresh air, warm clothing in cold weather, shelter, and many other necessities. Even our sexual desires stem from our need to express love and procreate the race.

Consider, second, our need for self-realization. Call it ego-status if you like, but each individual bears the image of God—with the power to think and to do. The need to be somebody is deeply rooted, for once again God made us that way.

Third, we need acceptance or "social approval." We need to feel loved, wanted, and needed. "None of us liveth to himself" (Romans 14:7). We were made that way too.

Fourth, life must have meaning in general and meaning for us personally. The human mind seems to inherently seek the answer to certain great questions. Where do we come

Understanding Ourselves

from? Why are we here? Where are we going? What is life all about? To truly live we must have enough to live *for* as well as enough to live *on*. We must have a sense of value. Those for whom life has lost its meaning often resort to suicide.

Then again, we have aesthetic needs —needs which only beautiful things can satisfy. In some people these needs seem more highly developed than in others, but beautiful flowers, white clouds in a blue sky, lovely music, meet a deep human need. I believe this distinguishes us from animals. I don't think a chimp gets anything out of a sunset, although it does respond to music. But for humans the need for the beautiful is inherent.

Finally, our spiritual needs top the list. We were made for fellowship with our Creator. We need someone above and beyond ourselves to tie to; "in him we live, and move, and have our being" (Acts 17:28).

You could make a different list, and it might be just as good. However, for purposes of analyzing human experience, these six needs are quite complete. Someone may say, "Is there not the need for security?" Yes, but when these needs are met, we feel secure. When they are not met, we feel frustrated, threatened, and insecure. One might also think of the need for new experiences, but as living creatures we need new experiences in all these areas.

Looking at ourselves now, with these needs in mind, and remembering that "none of us liveth to himself," notice that the character of all our relationships is formed in reference to these needs. We are attracted to people who satisfy these needs and repelled by people who threaten them.

A child, for example, becomes attracted to the first person who satisfies his needs. A good mother will not only meet his physical needs but will make him feel secure in a relationship which will meet all his needs in a balanced way.

You know how it is. You are drawn to people who make you feel that you are somebody, who welcome and accept you, who help bring meaning into your life. At the same time you are repelled by the people who do just the opposite. For example, how do you feel about a person who taunts, "You're nothing but a worm"?

On the playground a group of boys are talking about their dads. One boy's father designs great bridges. A lawyer's son tells about his father, who is the attorney on a case headlined in the current papers. Other boys boast of their dads' exploits. Some of the little fellows stand around with their eyes and mouths

Understanding Ourselves

open: "Look, he's somebody. Look who his dad is."

Now, let us assume that in the group is a little fellow who has no dad or whose father is a drunkard. Under these circumstances, he may manufacture wild tales about his dad. Why? Because he is a natural-born liar? No. To be somebody and to be accepted by the group seems to depend upon the exploits of fathers.

When God first created man, He provided for the fulfillment of all man's needs in a balanced way. Satan tempted Adam and Eve to satisfy these needs illegitimately and destructively, which resulted in sin and all that it has brought. One of the results of sin is unbalanced, distorted, and confused personalities so that sometimes one need eclipses the others.

Consider, for example, the need for self-realization and acceptance. Suppose I happen to be a little fellow who grew up in a home where I was not wanted. Even though but a child, I soon sense this, although I do not understand it. All through life I may be so hungry for acceptance and approval that I will do almost anything to get it.

The need for acceptance may be so great that a person cannot even afford to be himself. As a result, some people are very religious when they are with religious people, but when they are with irreligious people, they can be very irreligious. In order to be accepted, they think they need to play a particular role.

A person's need to feel accepted by everyone may be so great he cannot afford to take a position of his own, and, therefore, he finds it difficult to make decisions. He cannot afford to have a conviction of his own for fear of losing the favor of the majority.

God wants to supply all our needs according to the riches of His grace in Christ Jesus (Philippians 4:19), and that in a beautifully balanced way. Seeking to supply any one need at the expense of any of the others is really self-defeating. Recognizing that we are so conditioned, we need to examine ourselves in the light of these needs and also look at the basic law of life that makes for right relationships.

Selfishness Versus True Self-fulfillment

In all relationships, the law of life for earth and heaven is the law of self-sacrificing love. Nothing lives to itself. Let us go back to the illustration of the cell and its relation to other cells in the form of tissue. Suppose that one cell begins to live to itself and take nourishment to itself at the expense of the other cells. It begins to divide and subdivide all by itself and for its own sake irrespective of its place in the tissue. A mass grows, putting pressure on neighboring cells. What is happening? I'm sure you recognize, here, a tumor developing, and unless it is removed, it will quickly destroy the whole body, including itself. So when one person lives to himself and takes everything to himself at the expense of others, he definitely affects the welfare of all. Thus selfishness, self-centeredness, is the main cause of all strained and broken relationships.

Is it wrong to love oneself? By no means. Jesus said, "Thou shalt love thy neighbour *as thyself*" (Matthew 19:19). And our first duty to God and our fellow beings is that of self-development. Christ valued us so much that He gave up heaven and died for us. Surely, then, when we undervalue ourselves, we disappoint Him. God wants Christians to regard themselves as individuals of value, and our value is directly proportionate to the price God paid to save us. In fact, to truly love one's self is essential in order to truly love someone else. When self-respect leaves, respect for others lessens.

When, however, is a motive selfish? Don't you want to be saved for selfish reasons? When does self-love become selfishness? Perhaps the following diagram will help illustrate the difference between selfishness and true self-fulfillment. In it you see listed the six basic needs previously mentioned. The *I* on the left side represents me with all my needs. It doesn't take me long to realize that I need others to meet these needs and thus make me happy. But when I seek to meet my needs at the expense of others, I eventually discover that I am trapped in an ever-narrowing and self-destroying spiral.

Now note the *I* on the right. Here I am again with all the same needs. But when I recognize that other people have these needs, too, and begin to help meet their needs, I discover that my own needs are met. The spiral now keeps on widening, and I find in "others" a "we" concept.

21

Selfishness   True Self-fulfillment

Others   Spiritual   We
              Aesthetic
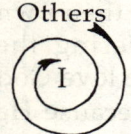   Meaning   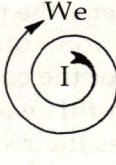
             Acceptance
        Self-realization
             Physical

I think this is what Jesus meant when He said, "Whosoever will save his life shall lose it; but whosoever shall lose his life for my sake and the gospel's, the same shall save it" (Mark 8:35). Here again the law of self-sacrificing love is the law of life for heaven and earth.

We are all born inherently selfish. Sin has made us all very self-centered. How can we make the transition from selfishness to true self-fulfillment? I think we can do it in four steps.

First, I love myself for my sake. This is pure selfishness. I think of everything only in terms of my needs and wishes. What will I get from this? Look what he did to me!

Second, I learn to love you, but for my sake. I need you to make me happy. This is an advance step because it provides another center around which my life can revolve. It is, however, still self-centered. Many never get beyond this second step. Even some parents who love their children love them only for their own sakes. When their children embarrass them, the parents think only of their own reputation, often without considering the needs of the children. Many people love God only in this way. They love Him because He forgives their sins, He answers their prayers, He protects them from harm, and He will give them a home in the earth made new. They love Him only because of what He will do for them, and when He doesn't answer their prayers as they think He should, they lose faith in Him and don't love Him anymore.

Third, as I mature, I learn to love you for your sake. I see value in you as a person. I love you for what you are, not just for what you can do for me. I begin to love my parents for their sakes. I begin to love God for His sake. I stand in awe at His marvelous wisdom and love and greatness as I see how He deals with the rebellion on this planet, and I come to appreciate Him for His sake.

Finally, I love myself for your sake—not so much for the happiness of the self as for the worth of the self. Happiness is the by-product. I now want to develop the best in me for your sake. I'll be the best father I can for the sake of my children, the best teacher for the sake of my students, the best pastor for the sake of my congregation, and the best person I can for

Selfishness Versus True Self-fulfillment

God's sake in order to make a better contribution to His cause.

Note the four steps: (1) I love myself for my sake, (2) I love you for my sake, (3) I love you for your sake, and (4) I love myself for your sake. The difference, then, between selfishness and true self-fulfillment is the difference between step one and step four.

Turn back to the diagram on page 21. If you put *S* in front of the *I* on the left side, and *N* after it, you have the word *SIN*. The diagram portrays what sin really is. Now in front of the *I* on the right side put the letters *CHR* and follow it with *ST*. This is what happens when a man takes Jesus Christ into his heart. Jesus does not destroy the self. He merely sets it free from selfishness and enables the person to develop his true self without being selfish. When this happens, all relationships take on new meaning and a new self emerges.

Self-denial

Someone just now may be thinking of Jesus' words in Luke 9:23: "If any man will come after me, let him deny himself, and take up his cross daily, and follow me." How can one develop his true self if he is to deny himself?

First, self-denial is not self-depreciation. Humility does not imply sadness. May I also remind you of what I said before: We should believe Heaven's estimate of our value. We should never put a low estimate upon ourselves or anyone else. God wants us to become like Jesus—like Himself.

What, then, does *self-denial* mean? It means we must refuse to satisfy our own desires or please or praise ourselves at the expense of others.

But what did Jesus mean when He said that we should take up our cross? We know something about what His cross was, but what is ours? Do our crosses consist merely of the heavy burdens we bear or the troubles we must carry?

Let us suppose that I should contract cancer. To spend the rest of my days in great pain would be a real cross for me to bear. Suppose we call in specialists who find a new way to treat the disease, and we call for the elders of the church, who anoint me with oil in the name of the Lord and pray for me (see James 5:14, 15). Let us say that in due time I completely recover my health and strength. Now what should I do? Jesus said I should carry my cross *daily*. Since I no longer have cancer, should I look around for some other trouble to carry? Of course not.

Some people carry a chip on their shoulders and think it is a cross. No, the only cross

Selfishness Versus True Self-fulfillment

Jesus asks us to carry is the one on which we must crucify our selfish hearts. Sometimes to deny ourselves the satisfaction of some strong desire seems like a crucifixion, but in reality that kind of cross leads to life.

Often we wrestle with these selfish desires of ours and find them too strong, and they overcome us. But we make our mistake in dealing with them negatively. We try to suppress them, ignore them, or continually fight them without success. Remember, all our desires have their roots in God-given needs. We must find ways and means of meeting these needs legitimately and constructively. In Christ we can develop our true selves without being selfish, which brings satisfaction. Instead of ignoring, suppressing, or fighting our desires, we should understand the basic underlying needs involved and deal with them positively. The apostle Paul wrote, "My God shall supply all your need according to his riches in glory by Christ Jesus" (Philippians 4:19).

Relationships Begin in the Home

Marriage is the most intimate of all human relationships. Here, if two people deliberately seek to meet each other's needs, they will find their own needs met with increasing satisfaction. Many divorces result from two egocentric adolescents eating each other and getting sick of the diet.

The process of "eating each other" can begin very subtly. If an insecure husband recognizes that his wife is more brilliant than he, his need for ego-status may cause him to belittle her in front of her friends. He does not realize that in so doing he is really defeating himself, for that kind of action really lowers him in the estimation of others. Should the husband praise his wife in front of her friends and let them know how much he appreciates her superior qualities, he would be surprised how his own ego-status as a husband would rise.

An insecure wife's need for acceptance of others may lead her to nag her husband about his faulty grammar or cause her to overspend

Relationships Begin in the Home

the family budget for clothing. And it will have the same effect.

The character or quality of personal relationships is determined largely in the home, for here people are conditioned to relate to others and to God. And right relationships with other persons are dependent upon a right relationship with God. There can be no true brotherhood of man without the Fatherhood of God.

To most people, God is but a big edition of daddy or some other authority figure. In fact, we often model our concept of God after our relationship with our parents. For example, a young woman around twenty years of age came into my office. "Pastor Heubach, I'm a most miserable person," she began. "I've tried to live a Christian life, but I know I won't make heaven; so why not just give up trying? Sometimes I think I'd like to go out into the world and live it up for a while and then end it all. I'm going to be lost anyway. But there's something inside me that won't let me do that. What can I do?"

Among other things, I suggested to her, "Tell me about yourself, Jane." In the course of our conversation I discovered that her mother was a perfectionist. (Let me say right here that it is not blame we are interested in but understanding.) Her mother was a very lovely person, but perfectionists find it difficult to live in an imperfect world. And sometimes it is hard to live with a perfectionist.

On one occasion the family had company. Since there were more people than beds, they moved some furniture to set up a space for sleeping bags. The travelers left early the next morning, the parents both went to work, and Jane—then about ten years old—went to school. The house was left in disorder as would be expected. For some reason school let out early that day, and when Jane came home, she decided to surprise her mother and straighten up the house. She put the furniture back where it belonged, picked up the used towels in the bathroom and put them in the laundry room, swept and dusted quickly in order to get as much done as possible before Mother returned from work.

Just as Jane put the finishing touches on the job, her mother came in, looked around, and noticed that in her haste Jane had not swept the corners very well and had forgotten to dust the rungs under the chairs. Then without a compliment or even a thank-you, Jane had to listen to a lecture on Whatever Is Worth Doing Is Worth Doing Well.

On another occasion Jane decided to fix supper. She set the table, prepared a meal she thought would be acceptable, and decided to

Relationships Begin in the Home

make biscuits—the first all by herself. She wept as she told me about it. "They were edible, too, Pastor Heubach." Do you know her mother's first words when she came into the kitchen? "Such a mess!" You see, in the process Jane had spilled some flour on the floor. Again there was no kiss of appreciation or words of commendation.

Now notice. Nothing Jane did seemed to be acceptable to her mother. Nothing was just right. Is it any wonder that ten years later as she sat in my office, nothing she did seemed quite right for God?

It is in the context of right relationships that life's blessings are mediated. And since these begin in the home, we all ought to give the home the priority it demands. It is here that all should study how more effectively to meet the needs of the others and how to bring out the best in each. Everyone has a unique personality, and we should recognize everyone as such and treat him as such. Each should understand the differences between selfishness and true self-fulfillment and that the law of love is the law of life for earth and heaven. The truth about God should be taught not only in word but in deed. Within such a home each can grow and mature into a person who knows peace and joy within himself even in the midst of problems.

What Is Love?

Since love is the law of life governing all healthy relationships, we should ask, "What is love?" Here are a few selections from the Bible: "The man who does not lead a good life is no son of God, nor is the man who fails to love his brother. For the original command, as you know, is that we should love one another. . . . My children, let us love not merely in theory or in words—let us love in sincerity and in practice! . . . To you whom I love I say, let us go on loving one another, for love comes from God. Every man who truly loves is God's son and has some knowledge of him. But the man who does not love cannot know him at all, for God is love. . . . Yes, we love him because he first loved us. If a man says, 'I love God' and hates his brother, he is a liar. For if he does not love the brother before his eyes how can he love the one beyond his sight? And in any case it is his explicit command that the one who loves God must love his brother too" (1 John 3:10, 11, 18; 4:7, 19, 20, Phillips).

We are all acquainted with these words of

What Is Love?

Jesus: "By this shall all men know that ye are my disciples, if ye have love one to another" (John 13:35).

Is love just an emotion, a feeling of warmth, of passion, of happiness, of fulfillment? If it is just a feeling, how can it be commanded? "This is my commandment," admonished Jesus, "That ye love one another" (John 15:12). An emotion is not a matter of command, intention, or demand. A feeling of love intentionally produced is artificial.

Many people insist, "Oh, I don't know, but I just don't love her anymore." Or, "I can't explain it, but I just don't love him anymore." Yet, love should have an enduring quality. Let me remind you of 1 Corinthians 13:4-8, again from Phillips: "This love of which I speak is slow to lose patience—it looks for a way of being constructive. It is not possessive: it is neither anxious to impress nor does it cherish inflated ideas of its own importance. Love has good manners and does not pursue selfish advantage. It is not touchy. It does not keep account of evil or gloat over the wickedness of other people. On the contrary, it is glad with all good men when truth prevails. Love knows no limit to its endurance, no end to its trust, no fading of its hope; it can outlast anything. It is, in fact, the one thing that still stands when all else has fallen."

If love "can outlast anything," why does some people's love fail? Love, then, must not be just an emotion, for our emotions are too unstable.

We often assume that intensity of feeling indicates the depth of love, but this is not necessarily the case. Consider, for example, two teen-agers who are very much "in love." Their feelings may be very intense for each other, but we would question the depth of their love because of their immaturity. The same holds true for extramarital relationships. Two people who have "an affair" may say that they are very much "in love" because their feelings for each other are intense. But feelings do not necessarily indicate the depth or maturity of love.

Is love, then, just a matter of ethics, a matter of obedience, a matter of being polite, courteous, thoughtful, or doing things that please someone else? Fear can prompt one to do all these things. A man in uniform rides a motorcycle up beside us and asks to see our driver's license. It is amazing how courteous and polite some of us get under such circumstances, and I am not so sure that we are always exhibiting love in such a case. Is love simply a principle by which we live, ignoring emotion?

Some people think of love in terms of being

What Is Love?

loved, rather than in terms of the capacity to love. The problem for them, then, is how to be loved—how to be lovable, popular, and appealing. For some, their theme song seems to be "Nobody Loves Me." Others seem to think of love in terms of an object rather than a faculty. To love is simply to find the right person to love and be loved by. We hear of people "falling in love," even at first sight. This cannot be adequate, because you can't fall in love with everybody, and the Christian should love everyone, even his enemies.

What, then, is love? In English, one word covers all aspects of this experience, but in classical Greek at least three words have been translated *love*. If we can understand this, it will help us see love in true perspective.

The word *eros* is sexual in nature, but it means much more. Erotic love refers to all kinds of physical ecstasy. One might even experience a heavenly *eros*. Perhaps you have listened to a symphony and have developed "goose pimples." This can be thought of as *eros*.

The word *philos* means friendly love—a love that friends experience with one another because they have many interests in common. It does not necessarily have sexual components. It is that love of good friends who share joys and sorrows together. Two boys who battled their way up some hill in Vietnam together are now buddies for life. This is *philos* love.

Finally, the word *agapē* refers to a principle—the principle of loyalty. Since it is something you deliberately do as an act of the will, it can, therefore, be commanded.

For two people in a marriage to have a love that never fails, they must have something more than a mere sexual attraction for each other. A marriage consummated purely on the basis of *eros* love will not last long if sickness or tragedy should make this relationship impossible.

People who really make a success of their marriage have many things they can do together besides making love on a physical level. This is where *philos* love comes in. Two people in love must also be good friends. They must have many things in common, many interests, many memories, many plans together on many levels. Such a love keeps two people together even though the physical aspect may be temporarily interfered with.

But the love that really holds a marriage together is *agapē* love. It is their decision to remain loyal to the marriage vows. They deliberately plan to act accordingly and to do the things that bring out the best in each other. *Agapē* love need never fail.

What Is Love?

Thus true love in a successful marriage really combines all three characteristics. There is physical attraction—sexual love—plus the love that shares many things in common, and also *agapē* love, which actually resembles God's love for us.

To truly understand love, we must understand it in the light of God's character and the nature of man. Man was created for fellowship with God and with his fellowmen, with God the center and source of life. Satan and man broke away from the center and became self-centered. This is sin, and it separated man from God and from his fellowman. Immediately Adam began to blame Eve. Soon Cain murdered Abel, and ever since, people have been separated from each other. Sin creates great gulfs and barriers, leaving man in loneliness, guilt, and anxiety.

The deepest need of man, then, is the need to overcome his separatedness, his loneliness, and his guilt. In every human heart remains the need to be one with his Creator and one with his fellowmen. Through Jesus, God brings about an atonement—"at-one-ment." Jesus prayed, "That they may be one, even as we are one" (John 17:22).

Love is the yearning for and the experiencing of oneness. Paul Tillich has put it this way: "Love is the drive towards the unity of the separated. Reunion presupposes separation of that which belongs essentially together. . . . But the estranged is striving for reunion. . . . Estrangement presupposes original oneness. Love manifests its greatest power there where it overcomes the greatest separation" (*Love, Power, and Justice*, p. 25).

Love, then, is not something which is added to life; rather, it is one of life's constituent elements. God made us that way.

The emotional quality of love—the feeling aspect of love—is but the joy of anticipation and experiencing of this reunion which takes place in every love relationship. The feeling aspect of love is the by-product of what love really is. And when people confuse the by-product with the real thing, they think that everything is gone when the results are gone. "I looked to Jesus," said Spurgeon, "and the dove of peace sang in my heart. I looked at the dove, and it flew away." Think about that a moment. Too many people confuse the dove with Jesus.

The different kinds of love express our desire for union on different levels of living and in different relationships. Love is the moving power of life itself. "We know that we have passed from death unto life, because we love the brethren. He that loveth not his brother abideth in death" (1 John 3:14). No love, no life. Love, or perish. Let me repeat again my definition. True love is the yearning for and experiencing of oneness with God and man.

Now to meet this need for oneness, Satan and man have devised many pseudo means to escape from this separatedness. I like the way Erich Fromm in his book *The Art of Loving* analyzes them. Take, for example, the *orgiastic trances of heathen rituals* and their more sophisticated counterparts in some of the dances that you observe. "In a transitory state of exaltation the world outside disappears, and with it the feeling of separateness from it. Inasmuch as these rituals are practiced in common, an experience of fusion with the group is added which makes this solution all the more effective" (p. 11). As the participants engage in rhythmic swings, hand clapping, and contortions together, they become one with the group. And this lifts them out of their loneliness, but when the group breaks up, then what?

Consider *alcoholism and drug addiction*. Drugs can give the feeling of oneness. Suddenly you find an escape from loneliness, frustration, and the problems of guilt, fear, and anxiety. Under their influence you may feel like you love everybody. The tragedy is that you "feel all the more separate after the . . . experience is over, and thus are driven to take recourse to it with increasing frequency and intensity" (p. 12), which, in turn, is followed with even greater frustration and more loneliness.

Sexual promiscuity does the same thing. The fusion here is only partial. It takes complete oneness, complete commitment, for true fusion, and partial, illegitimate union makes complete oneness difficult if not impossible, for it violates the integrity of the individual. The two only use each other. You cannot completely commit yourself to more than one person.

Union based on conformity is another example. "If I am like everybody else, if I have no feelings or thoughts which make me different, if I conform in custom, dress, ideas to the pattern of the group, I am saved . . . from the frightening experience of aloneness" (p. 13). But here, also, I gain this at the expense of my own integrity. I therefore can have no convictions, no insights of my own. And this can lead only to frustration.

Again, *one can drown his loneliness in activity*. Here one experiences a sort of oneness with work. If I can't seem to get along with people, I can lose myself in my job. In my manipulation of certain gadgets, I become one with them, which gives me only an inadequate satisfaction, for objects are impersonal.

What Is Love?

A *continual craving for amusements* reveals the deep longings of the soul, but those who drink at the fountain of worldly pleasure will also find their soul-thirst still unsatisfied.

A *very passive, dependent person* tries to escape "the unbearable feeling of isolation and separateness by making himself part and parcel of another person who directs him, guides him, protects him" (p. 19). He thus "does not have to make decisions, does not have to take any risks; he is never alone" (p. 19), and so he becomes a parasite on another. This is not adequate either, because he has no personal integrity. If something should happen to the other person or if the other person should fail him, then what?

The *domineering person* does the same thing "by making another person part and parcel of himself. . . . [He] commands, exploits, hurts, humiliates, and the . . . [other] person is commanded, exploited, hurt, and humiliated" (p. 20) for the same reason.

All these methods of fusion seem to hold some promise of escaping our feelings of separatedness, our loneliness, but they are false because they are only partial fulfillments and ignore the integrity of the individual. All such pseudo means seek union apart from the Center and Source of life, God our Creator.

True Christian love, then, is not just an

emotion, but a dynamic force in life involving the whole person and every phase of life. In fact, it is the moving force of life.

Christian love is primarily giving rather than receiving. The selfish person thinks of giving only in terms of being deprived of something or in terms of giving in exchange for something. If he gives without receiving, he feels cheated. To this kind of person the expression "It is better to give than to receive" means "It is better to suffer deprivation than to experience joy." And, of course, he completely misunderstands what Jesus meant.

You see, everything in nature that is healthy and alive *gives*. We, too, need to learn that loving is giving. Jesus pointed out to the woman of Samaria that should she find the true center of her life she would have a well of water within instead of a broken cistern. Some people are like broken cisterns. (Cisterns are large containers for collecting and storing rainwater.) If the cistern should crack, the rainwater would leak out and spider webs might begin to form. Maybe even some dead frogs would be found inside. Then the cistern would need cleaning out, patching, and refilling. Now, some people are like that. They are never happy unless someone continues to pour in happiness. After a while it all leaks out, and inside they find the dead frogs of

What Is Love?

envy and jealousy, the spider webs of pity and despair.

Other people resemble bubbling fountains, always overflowing. We enjoy being in their company. Jesus pointed out that if we get back to our True Center—get in touch with the Source of life—we shall within then become, not broken cisterns that always need to be filled but bubbling fountains continually overflowing, bringing joy and happiness to other people.

For the person who understands, who is no longer a slave to himself, and who finds his true center in God, "giving is the highest expression of . . . [life]. In the very act of giving, I experience my strength," my will, and my purpose for living. "This experience fills me with joy. . . . Giving is more glorious than receiving, not because it is a deprivation, but because in the act of giving lies the expression of my aliveness" (p. 23). Everything in nature that is healthy and alive does the very same thing.

I think one of the greatest tragedies of poverty is not so much what one is unable to buy or the suffering one experiences because he is poor. I think the greatest tragedy of poverty is that it keeps one from experiencing the joy of giving. A person who is so poor that he always has to think about how he is going to get his next meal has a harder time experiencing the joy of sharing with others.

True Christian love, then, involves many things: concern, responsibility, respect, loyalty, agreement, appreciation, and sensitivity to needs.

Love and Conflict

But someone might ask, "Does love mean the absence of conflict?" If two people argue and fight, how can they be motivated by Christian love? Can people have conflicts and still love each other?

It is strange that in many of our homes where love should be its best, where it carries its greatest potential, there is bickering and fighting and arguing. It seems that some have a hard time being kind to those they love most, and yet they can be marvelously polite and loving to people they scarcely know. What about it?

Does love mean the absence of conflict? Not necessarily. If down deep in their hearts the longing for oneness still remains, their case is not hopeless. Then why the conflicts? Many conflicts are actually attempts to avoid real conflicts. Disagreements on minor and superficial matters do not lend themselves to clarification or solution, but most people are afraid to get at the real source of the trouble. So

What Is Love?

they cover it up with fights over trivialities.

I have heard people argue over such insignificant matters as how to squeeze the toothpaste tube. A man being an engineer, of course, needs to squeeze it from the bottom to maintain contour of the tube all the way. The woman picks it up anywhere and squeezes it, and the poor toothpaste tube becomes distorted. This can cause a big family argument. But is a little tube of toothpaste a matter of sufficient weight to break up a home? No. Many of the conflicts among those who love each other are simply disagreements on superficial matters, and because the two are both afraid to get at the real source of the trouble, they "cover it up" with toothpaste!

Real conflicts between two people, those which do not serve to cover up but which lead to clarification, produce a catharsis from which both persons emerge with more knowledge and a closer understanding of each other. This can lead to the more complete unity for which they both long. Unfortunately, many refuse to face the truth about themselves.

Love is possible only if two people communicate with each other from the center of their hearts. The presence of conflicts may mean merely the absence of communication. Indeed, most of us communicate on such a shallow level that we never get through to each other, never really learn to know each other.

Love is not merely a resting-place in paradise, but the moving, growing, working together toward oneness. Because two people are very different, to bring about this union is difficult and takes a lifetime.

Agapē love, which is an act of the will, enables us to love even our enemies. We can thus learn to love people we don't like. With this understanding in mind, we don't have to feel guilty about lacking feelings of ecstasy in our relationship with some people who are very difficult to love. We all know it is pretty hard to love people who are unlovely. But in *agapē* love, it is not necessary to have a romantic feeling for them. You do not even need to have many things in common with them. You can, however, have a relationship with them which grows out of an understanding of human nature and which enables you to see them as children of our heavenly Father—see them as people with basic needs and as individuals who are unlovely because of certain factors in their past lives which have made them that way.

Love Must Be Cultivated

Agapē love does not just come naturally. We must cultivate it. This kind of love, you see, is a faculty to be exercised and not just

What Is Love?

something to be experienced ecstatically. The ability to love, like other abilities and skills, is a fine art. Erich Fromm in his book *The Art of Loving* points out that like any other art, the art of loving requires a number of things. One important factor is theory. If you want to master the piano or some other musical instrument, you need to know a certain amount of theory. In fact, the more theory you understand, the better background you will have and the better you are prepared to become a master. But it takes more than a knowledge of the theory involved. It takes a great deal of discipline, concentration, and patience. There must also be supreme concern—magnificent obsession, if you please—to master any art. And then it takes practice, many hours a day. Often little passages—difficult passages—must be practiced over and over and over again.

Could we then think that the art of loving should call for less? The better we understand the theory of love, the better we are prepared to learn how to love. But in learning how to love in the truest sense of the word, it takes discipline, concentration, and patience. We must have a supreme concern to master the art of loving and plan to practice *agapē* love in all relationships. But we cannot do it successfully on our own.

Sometimes people think they can't learn to love as Christ loved because they find it hard to love their enemies. They forget that the ability to love the unlovely is not a prerequisite to fellowship with Christ or something we must develop on our own in order to be Christians. Rather, it grows as a result of our fellowship with Christ. When Jesus was talking to Peter, He didn't say, "Peter, do you love people?" No, He said, "Peter, do you love *Me?*"

Love for Jesus enables us to see people as He sees them—to recognize them as children of our heavenly Father just as we are. We can then deliberately try to relate to them as we think God wants us to. In the context of such a relationship with Jesus Christ, we can become more lovely and can better share Christ's love with others.

I don't know if you have had the experience yourself, but I am sure you have known of once-bitter enemies becoming good friends. It is what Jesus meant when He said, "This is my commandment, That ye love one another" (John 15:12). We can learn to love in fellowship with the Saviour.

No Love Without Communication

There can be no love without fellowship, and there can be no fellowship without communication. By communication, of course, I mean more than simply speaking the same language. I mean getting through to each other on the deeper levels of life. When communication breaks down, satisfying relationships become impossible.

Have you ever wondered why we find communication so difficult? At least three egocentric predicaments make it so.

First of all, we can be preoccupied with self. I can be so absorbed with my own thoughts that I do not hear a word you say, even though I may appear to be listening. I may look straight at you, yet my mind can be a thousand miles away. Some problem, some decision I must make, some anticipated or past experience, may so absorb my mind as to make it practically impossible for you to get through to me in any way. We may even actually argue some point with someone else and still not be listening. While you give your views, I may be thinking about my next point or how I can prove you wrong.

Second, there is the problem of semantics. Words can mean different things to different people because of their differing backgrounds. The word *bay*, for example, apart from any context, will call to mind many different pictures in any group of people. Some would think of a body of water. Others, perhaps, of a bay tree or bay leaves. Still others of a bay horse, bay windows, or hounds that bay. Of course, the sentence in which the word occurs would help, but many words convey different meanings to different people even in their context.

I am not speaking of dictionary meanings alone, but meanings in terms of past experiences, for words carry emotional content as well. One may have a good feeling through and through when he hears a certain word, while another may hear the same word and feel very sad.

As a result, we need to be good listeners and seek to understand what words mean to other people in order to communicate with them. I learned this lesson at a clinic in Los Angeles. A woman suffering from schizophrenia came to the clinic for treatment. At times she was so separated from reality that she could not do her housework. Because she

No Love Without Communication

was a very religious person, the doctor thought that I might help her and referred her to my office.

One day as we were talking, she seemed to be unusually lucid and normal in her thinking, so in the course of our conversation, I remarked, "You seem to have difficulty in coming to grips with reality, don't you?"

She replied, "That's it, that's exactly it, that's what I need. If only I could come to grips with reality!" And her thoughts seemed to go a million light-years away.

Now, what did I mean by the word *reality*? Being a good farm boy, reality to me was coming to grips with the demands of the day—the activities that needed attention now, such as doing the chores. For some women, *reality* means taking care of the children, dealing with the little problems of life as they come along—seeing things as they are. But do you know what the word *reality* meant to her? She had read a great deal in the field of metaphysics, and to her the only reality in the universe was the *Essence of the Divine Mind*. Coming to grips with reality meant to come to grips with the Essence of the Divine Mind. That counseling session ended there so far as any further communication was concerned.

We see things and hear things as *we* are, not as *they* are. Two people can use the same terms and might even engage in a great discussion and still not really communicate. Sometimes after arguing for a time they finally decide to define their terms. One will say, "Oh, if that's what you mean, that's different." We should make sure that we understand and make clear what we mean by the words we use and find out as soon as possible what they mean to those with whom we wish to communicate.

The third predicament that makes communication difficult is the *mask* each wears, the facade he hides behind, the games or roles he plays with others. If I am immature and insecure, I feel that I will need to play certain roles in my relationship with others in order for them to accept me. For example, I am a minister and a Bible teacher. When I talk with you, if I am insecure I must wear the ministerial mask and talk as I expect that you think ministers ought to talk. I can't afford to let you see what I really am and what I really think down deep in my heart. You might discover that I am human. Ministers, you see, are supposed to be divine, not human (or are they?).

Some people play games so well and wear masks so much of the time that they themselves actually forget who they really are. Perhaps you have read Helen Haiman Joseph's poem:

No Love Without Communication

The Mask

Always a mask
Held in a slim hand, whitely,
Always she had a mask before her face—
Smiling and sprightly,
The mask.

Truly the wrist
Holding it lightly
Fitted the task:
Sometimes however
Was there a shiver,
Fingertip quiver,
Ever so slightly—
Holding the mask?

For years and years and years I wondered
But dared not ask.

And then—
I blundered,
I looked behind,
Behind the mask,
To find
Nothing—
She had no face.

She had become
Merely a hand
Holding a mask
With grace.

—From *The Saturday Review of Literature.*

We should not condemn the wearing of masks altogether. They are helpful at times. Were we not able to wear them, there might be no communication at all. Teen-agers on their first date may feel insecure in their relationships to begin with (and this is not limited to the teens) and so put on their best behavior. Masks may provide a valuable aid for a while. Like crutches, they serve a temporary purpose. But we should grow in our communicative skills and try to create an atmosphere in which we can safely take off our masks and be what we really are. As we become more mature and secure, we don't need to play games with each other, we don't need to wear masks. We can be our true selves.

Life's Blessings Are Mediated in the Context of Fellowship

"One winter evening Ole Bull, the great violinist, was traveling across the prairie in the dead of winter, and became lost in a blizzard, about fifteen miles from the nearest farmhouse, twenty miles from the nearest town. The storm had blown down the guideboards, and having completely lost his way, Ole Bull let his big gray horse take his own course.

"Thus he pressed on through the storm, not knowing the direction of his going, nor where he could find shelter. Then when hope was dead and life was ebbing in that awful cold, he saw, across the fenceless prairie, a faint, twinkling light, gleaming dimly like a lighthouse above a blinding sea.

"The light disappeared, and he thought it must have been but a vision of his troubled brain; and then it came, and he saw that it was a light from a window. When he came to the place, he tried the door, but found it locked. There was no word or sign of welcome. Ole put his horse in a ruined cattle shed. . . .

"Soon a light shone from the suddenly opened door. A terrible creature stood holding a lantern that threw strange shadows. He uttered fierce imprecations.

" 'Get you gone, whoever you be;
   For I've sealed an oath in heaven, never
      human face to see;
   Heart and soul to hate abandoned, love
      by cruel torture wronged,
   I've renounced for years, forever, all that
      to my life belonged.
   Take your way; begone! ay, perish in yon
      wild demoniac yeast;
   For the wrong that I have suffered I will
      have revenge at least.'

"Ole Bull seized the mad hermit by the shoulder, and led him back into the cabin with a grip like a vise.

" 'I am here to stay till morning, asking
      neither food nor grace;
   Sit you here within the shadow, and I
      charge you keep your place.'

"Sat they hours thus in silence, and the
   hermit crooning low
Took a fiddle from a cupboard, woke
   the airs of long ago.

"Ole wondered at the caprice of the hermit, and though he realized that the man had but little art or skill, yet he sensed that the strains came from the lonely creature's heart. The old hermit played for a long time as though unconscious of Ole. Then, with a cold and feigned politeness and with bitter jest, the well-bred irony telling of better days sometime in the hermit's past, the madman asked Ole if he would not lay aside his cloak and play.

"Ole swept aside his cloak, rose and took the fiddle. He said in after days, telling of it, that never before had he felt the all-conscious power of his art within him. Then, as he played, he saw visions panoramic of applauding galleries, the glowing transport swelling from thousands of hearts. He felt the thrill of emotion that starts the tear of rapture. And all that gilded pageant was in Ole's playing for one single lonely heart.

"Ole broke into the strains of 'Home, Sweet Home.' The hermit rose, approached Ole and looked him searchingly in the face. He wondered if the violinist were not an angel that had come to visit him unawares. As the hermit gazed in wonder, the tears wet the lashes of his eyes as they overflowed with moisture.

"And next, the music softly stealing

seemed to the hermit as his mother's long-forgotten prayers. The long pent-up tears coursed down the care-worn features of the old hermit. . . . Like the waters of Meribah made sweet, this man's hard nature was softened, his bitterness of spirit was healed under music's wondrous spell. The spring flowed once more in the desert of the soul. . . .

"After that the two men could lie side by side on the narrow cot that was now made wide by their new-found friendship.

" 'Saved, ay, saved,' the hermit murmured,
   'I have found my life again;
Found a deeper, truer meaning in the
   words, my fellow men.' " *

The story of Ole Bull and the hermit brings to my mind the truth expressed in Psalm 133: "Behold, how good and how pleasant it is for brethren to dwell together in unity! It is like the precious ointment upon the head, that ran down upon the beard, even Aaron's beard: that went down to the skirts of his garments; as the dew of Hermon, and as the dew that descended upon the mountains of Zion: for there the Lord commanded the blessing, even life for evermore."

---

*From *Buried Treasure*, by Lucas A. Reed, pp. 142, 143.

The Context of Fellowship

When I first read Psalm 133, I thought that the antecedent of the word *there* in the third verse (where it says "for there the Lord commanded the blessing, even life for evermore") was Mount Zion. But as I studied the psalm I decided that the antecedent is in the first verse. Moffatt translates it: *"In this fellowship has the Eternal fixed the blessing of an endless life."* The Lord commanded life forevermore where people dwell together in unity.

The atmosphere of fellowship which men enjoy resembles a rare perfume and is as refreshing as dew upon the grass. In the context of fellowship, life's blessings are mediated.

Similarly, it is in the context of fellowship that we can comprehend spiritual truths most effectively. That is why Jesus could declare, "I *am* the truth. Come unto *Me*." That is why the Bible is a book of men, not just a series of abstract theories. Even in the realm of abstract ideas, discussion in an atmosphere of fellowship always brings new insights when minds are alert. We can all agree with Edgar Guest that we would "rather see a sermon than hear one any day."

"There is an eloquence far more powerful than the eloquence of words in the quiet, consistent life of a pure, true Christian. What a man is has more influence than what he says. . . .

"No other influence that can surround the human soul has such power as the influence of an unselfish life. The strongest argument in favor of the gospel is a loving and lovable Christian" (*The Ministry of Healing*, pp. 469, 470).

In the context of fellowship the Lord has commanded the blessing of spiritual insights. He made us that way. That is why He had such close fellowship with His disciples, and in that fellowship they caught a vision of spiritual truths which affected their entire lives.

Fellowship arouses dormant faculties and calls them into action. It inspires us to great achievements. All of us will testify, I believe, that the greatest influence in our lives was that exerted upon us by some person, however humble he may have been. That is why God asks people to share the gospel. In the context of fellowship, people are inspired.

Fellowship also breaks down barriers, dispels prejudices, and clarifies misunderstandings. Have you ever felt that a specific person seemed to have an impenetrable wall about him? He seemed to possess no human sympathy or understanding but lived aloof from common people like yourself. And then when circumstances beyond your control have thrown you into his company, you have found that somehow the walls disintegrated, and

The Context of Fellowship

you gradually came to realize that he, too, was human.

Notice, too, that in the context of fellowship, faith and love and all the other aspects of the "fruit of the Spirit" develop, and men are changed—transformed. These Christian graces are the by-products of fellowship with Christ, not prerequisites to that fellowship. Many people get the idea that they must develop faith, love, patience, and self-control before they can have fellowship with Christ. But Paul calls these graces "the *fruit* of the Spirit," not the *"prerequisites* to the baptism of the Holy Spirit." In our fellowship with Jesus, the Holy Spirit takes possession of us and transforms us.

Again, in the context of fellowship, prayer becomes more meaningful. Have you experienced the discouragement of seemingly unanswered prayers? Someone has suggested, "God always answers prayer with either Yes or No or Wait awhile," which implies that prayer is only a matter of petitions or requests to be granted, denied, or postponed. But is your only conversation with someone you love a matter of requesting favors? No! Friends in fellowship share many experiences. One can enjoy fellowship with a friend even in silence. God tells us, "Be still, and know that I am God" (Psalm 46:10).

If prayer means talking with God as with a friend, then many prayers do not even need answering. Why? Because they have become experiences of sharing interests, joys, and sorrows together. Jesus promised, "Where two or three are gathered together in my name, there am I in the midst of them" (Matthew 18:20). Prayer becomes meaningful in an atmosphere of fellowship, for there the Lord has commanded the blessing of communion.

Furthermore, fellowship strengthens us with courage. The Greek word used in Matthew 5:4 for comfort means literally "to call to one's side." When Jesus spoke the words "Blessed are they that mourn: for they shall be comforted," He could have meant that they would be strengthened by fellowship. "Fear thou not," God said, "for I am with thee" (Isaiah 41:10). And the response of the believing Christian is: "I will fear no evil: for thou art with me."

Human as well as divine fellowship encourages and strengthens us. We take courage and develop greater strength to resist temptation when we know someone is with us. Jesus sent out His disciples two by two so they could encourage each other. It's easy to get discouraged when you find yourself standing alone. Even Jesus longed for human fellowship in the hour of His deepest agony!

The Heart of Christianity

When you think of it, do not relationships constitute the heart of Christianity? The religion of Christ is a satisfying, personal love relationship with God and with each other in the midst of an intense conflict between good and evil. Christianity is more a relationship to a person—God, Christ, your neighbor—than subscription to a creed, for doctrine is important only as it affects relationships. What you believe about God affects your relationship to Him—whether you serve Him from fear, duty, or love. A study of doctrine is a study of how God deals with man and with the problem of sin. It tells us what kind of God He is and how He relates to His universe. Jesus said, "This is life eternal, that they might know thee the only true God, and Jesus Christ, whom thou hast sent" (John 17:3). To know Him means to love Him.

The matter of relationships helps us better understand sin and salvation. We should think of sin in terms of broken relationships—first with God and then with each other. Salvation restores these relationships.

Christian love is the longing for and experiencing of fellowship and reunion—the kind of reunion which preserves one's own individuality and enhances it. It means finding the best in others while developing our true selves without being selfish. Such love seeks God's glory and not our own. It emphasizes giving rather than receiving. It bridges the gulf that separates us from God and our fellowman.